My Dog Changed My Life

H. Norman Wright

Paintings by Jim Lamb

HARVEST HOUSE PUBLISHERS

EUGENE, OREGON

My Dog Changed My Life

Text Copyright © 2004 by H. Norman Wright
Published by Harvest House Publishers
Eugene, Oregon 97402

Library of Congress Cataloging-in-Publication Data

Wright, H. Norman.
  My dog changed my life / by H. Norman Wright.
    p. cm.
  ISBN 0-7369-1148-0 (alk. paper)
  1. Dogs. 2. Human-animal relationships. I. Title.
  SF426.2.W76 2004
  636.7'0887--dc21

                    2003013264

Artwork designs are copyrighted by Jim Lamb and may not be reproduced without the artist's permission.
For information regarding art prints, art cards, and mini prints featured in this book, please contact:

Jim Lamb   For limited edition prints:
1604 217th Place SE   Wild Wings, Inc.
Sammamish, WA 98075   (800) 445-4833
E-mail: plainair2@comcast.net   www.wildwings.com
Website: www.jimlambstudio.com

Design and production by Koechel Peterson & Associates, Inc.,
Minneapolis, Minnesota

Harvest House Publishers and the author have made every effort to trace the ownership of all poems and quotes. In the event of a question arising from the use of a poem or quote, we regret any error made and will be pleased to make the necessary correction in future editions of this book.

Printed in China.

06 07 08 09 10 11 12 / LP / 10 9 8 7 6

Life-Altering Friendships

A dog: companion, friend, protector, playmate, and life-changer! Dogs add a dimension to our lives that otherwise would be just a vacant spot. They work for us, guard us, play with us, and keep us company. It's true. Having a dog will change your life more than you ever dreamed! Just think about it for a moment…

Does your dog fit into your schedule or could it be the other way around?

Do you have to get a dog sitter before you can leave for a weekend?

Do you have to be home at a specific time to feed or potty your dog?

Do you have to take time off work to take your pooch to the vet?

Do you rush out to clean the lawn so your gardener can cut the grass?

Is it your idea to walk around the block each night at 9:30 P.M. with a dog stopping every five feet to smell and mark his spot?

No, because dogs cause us to reschedule our lives. And that's all right. These are just a few of the many learning experiences that come with owning a dog. They change our lives in so many ways. ❧

A dog is one of the remaining reasons why some people can be persuaded to go for a walk.

O. A. BATTISTA

Dog on the Street Interview

Dogs laugh, but they laugh with their tails.

Max Eastman

I'm sure you've seen a "Man on the Street" interview. Well, one day I decided to do something totally different. I set out to conduct a "Dog on the Street" interview. I left my home and walked over to the park where I knew some of the canine clan would be. I motioned to one alert pup to come over and he complied. I set up my tape recorder and asked him if he would mind if I interviewed him. He was very obliging. I said, "Dogs lead an interesting life, I'm sure there are things you could share with me that we humans don't know."

I could see him thinking and then he smiled and said, "Bet you didn't know there's a museum dedicated to dogs."

"Nope, never heard of it," I said.

"Yup. It's in St. Louis. It's called the American Kennel Club Museum of the Dog. It's nestled on 300 acres and is filled with 2,000 pieces of art inspired by dogs. If you're ever in the area, stop by and check out the collection of silver and brass dog collars. I've heard it's pretty nice. And don't forget to send me a postcard. *I'm trying to develop a better relationship with our mail carrier.*"

I said, "Ah, I'll try to remember that. Anything else that's earth-shattering news?"

"Yeah, let me tell you something else about us. Did you know we dogs have a star named after us? *No, it's not on the Hollywood Walk of Fame.* It's Sirius, the Dog Star. When the Romans ruled, they called the hottest weeks in summer 'the dog days.' They thought the placement of the star had something to do with the heat. It doesn't, but, hey, it goes to prove humans aren't always right."

"Well sometimes we aren't—so what else do we need to know since there are so many dogs in this country?"

"In modern-day China dogs are rare. Overcrowding has led to restrictions on pet ownership and many pet lovers are forced to visit zoos just to see us, or they can even rent us by the hour."

"Rent dogs?"

"Yes, in Japan. Did you know many Japanese dog lovers actually resort to buying robotic dogs? And, let me tell you, robotic dogs are not cheap. Each electronic wonder costs about $2,000. But at least the owners save money on dog food, which in Japan, is mostly made of fish…Yuck!"

"Do you enjoy humans?"

"Yeah, they're okay but humans actually prefer us. Spending time with us dogs is something humans all over the world like to do. But I must admit, I was pleasantly surprised when the dog across the street told me that an American Animal Hospital Association poll found that 57 percent of pet owners surveyed would choose to be shipwrecked on a desert island with their pet than with another person."

"Hmm…really?"

"Yup, the dog across the street also told me about a dog by the name of Randy who didn't have to be shipwrecked to face a watery ordeal. He fell into a neighbor's Doughboy pool and had to tread water for at least 18 hours before being found. *Talk about dog paddling!*"

"Ohh…," I groaned at the pun.

"Since we're on the subject of pools, did you know that a lot of dogs own their own wading pools? You know the ones I'm talking about—those blue, hard plastic ones for kids. Nothing beats lying in one filled with cool water on a hot summer day."

(I couldn't get a word in edgewise once he got started).

"Here's another item from the 'hard-to-believe' file: For $10,000, you can have my DNA frozen and stored so I can be cloned in the future. *All I ask is that you don't forget to pay the $100 annual storage fee!*"

"Oh, I don't think so, but thanks for all this info. By the way, do you play Trivial Pursuit?"

"No, why do you ask?"

"No reason you'd understand. Thanks again." ❧

Dogged Determination

Rosella didn't just change her owner's life—she saved it. She is a guide dog who serves Michael Hingston who is blind. They were in the Twin Towers on September 11. When the first plane struck, she hurried to Michael's side. He said, "She knew something was different. But she never freaked out and never lost her focus."

From the 78th floor, Rosella brought Michael down the stairwell one step at a time. She would step down, wait for Michael, then step down again, and wait. Somewhere around the 25th floor, they were exhausted and someone handed out bottles of water. They stopped briefly for this and then continued down step by step. About an hour after the plane hit, they reached the ground floor and scrambled to safety.

Just imagine all of the bedlam, chaos, hysteria, heat, and smoke. How did this dog ignore all the distraction, noise, and frantic people? There are two character qualities in Rosella that would serve us well in our life. She had discipline for her job and devotion for her master.

Are we that disciplined for what we're called to do? And are we that devoted to our Master? It's something to think about. 🐾

Sincerely Yours

Many times we close our letters with the phrase "sincerely yours." But are we really? Humans have the ability to fake sincerity. A dog cannot. Roger Caras said, "A dog is utterly sincere. It cannot pretend...People use you and pretend they don't while dogs use you in complete honesty because they have no choice, and they have not an ounce of deceit in their soul nor self-consciousness about any of this."

We may repress our feelings. Our dog doesn't. We may lie about our feelings. Our dog can't and won't. Perhaps that's one of the reasons why we're so drawn to dogs. Maybe our dog is telling us a better way to live. 🐾

Don't accept your dog's admiration as conclusive evidence that you are wonderful.

ANN LANDERS

George the Paperdog

One day I decided it would be nice if George learned to fetch the morning newspaper. I walked down the driveway with George at my side and began to make over the paper without picking it up.

Always fascinated with whatever I showed any interest in, George playfully attacked the paper. He stepped on it, rolled over it, and eventually picked it up and dared me to take it away from him. Verbally, I praised him and began to coax him toward the house with the paper. He didn't see the point of this game and quickly dropped the paper when I called. We repeated the same scenario half a dozen times before George finally got the paper all the way to the front porch.

The next morning, we went through the whole ritual again. By the third day, George had made the connection. A slightly chewed paper was waiting for me on the porch that morning. I hugged him. I praised him. I gave him a treat. "Way to go, George!"

Now there are many things in life you need just one of. One wife is a good thing. Two isn't. One watch is just fine, but if you wear two, you no longer know the exact time. And unless you plan to line a lot of birdcages, one morning newspaper is more than sufficient.

There's an old saying, "Give a boy a hammer and everything becomes a nail." A similar truth holds for dogs: "Teach a dog to fetch a paper, and all paper routes soon lead to your front door."

At first it wasn't much of a problem. I opened the front door and found George with not only our paper, but also our next-door neighbor's paper. "Uh…good dog. You want a treat, right? Sure, only leave the Bottoms' paper alone next time." No big deal. An easy toss back to their driveway. The following day,

George faithfully retrieved half a dozen neighbors' papers. My daily ritual took on some modifications of its own. An extra five minutes was added to my morning to rede-liver the slightly chewed papers to the neighbors.

Soon George had branched out to the next block and had taken to following the newspaper boy on his route. Neighbors began call-ing to ask for their papers.

My four-legged kleptomaniac had a full-blown compulsion. He was a newspaper junkie with a fetish for fetching.

It took weeks to detox George and return him to his pre-fetching old self. 🐾

Pet Therapy

No matter how little money and how few possessions you own, having a dog makes you rich.

Louis Sabin

What is the impact of the presence of pets on families undergoing a life crisis? Studies showed the presence of companion animals, especially cats and dogs, had a beneficial impact on the adult caregiver while caring for a spouse who had cancer. Parents reported that pets helped them feel better when sad. A surprising number felt that pet care was not a burden, even though they were caring for their spouse. Adults who were terminally ill frequently remarked that their pets were important in helping them cope when they felt distressed during their illness by providing them a reason to live, consistent companionship, and affection.

The companionship of pets (particularly dogs) helped children in families adjust better to the serious illness and sudden death of a parent. The benefits were observed in five areas: Children received love at a time when their need for love was enormous; children were able to confide their feelings more readily to their pets than to people; taking care of their pets helped maintain structure in the midst of a vast disruption in their daily routines; children felt competent by taking care of the pet at a time when their lives felt out of control; and children felt needed by their pet. ❀

The Heroes Among Us

Sophie looked like any other Dalmatian except there was one difference—she was deaf. So she couldn't hear five-year-old Georgia's screams when the child fell into a raging river. However, Sophie saw her struggling and without hesitating she plunged into the water and swam out to her. The little girl grabbed onto Sophie's neck and she paddled back to the bank. What a welcome they both received from Georgia's mother. Sophie had won a place in their hearts forever.

On the flipside, it's not much fun being a stray. There's no master to love or care for you. You have to scrounge for food; other dogs and even people pick on you. It's easy to become suspicious, wary, and self-absorbed. One day a stray dog found a plastic bag under a picnic table during a frigid winter day and began to stand guard over it. When he saw people, he began to bark and howl until they came over to see what the disturbance was about it. When the bag was opened, they found a baby girl stuffed inside with her umbilical cord still attached. The baby was rushed to a hospital where she recovered. The stray dog? The maternity unit of the hospital adopted him. ❖

Move It!

*The dog has got
more fun out of
man than man
has got out of the
dog, for man is the
more laughable of
the two animals.*

JAMES THURBER

Your dog can improve your health. Imagine that you are a dog owner who experiences a heart attack. You are eight times more likely to survive the first year after the attack than those who don't own a dog.

How's the exercise factor in your life? Does it exist? If not, get a dog. Too many folks live a morbid sedentary lifestyle while the pounds add up. If you own a dog, your shift from the couch to the outdoors may be dramatic. Your walking time, as well as number of outings, will increase significantly. Your dog could be credited with saving your life and helping your family be more healthy. ❧

If You Want Brighter Children, Get a Dog

A dog can have more of an impact on your child's development in a positive manner than anyone realizes. A child who helps raise an animal is better at decoding body language and understanding others' feelings and motives. He has more empathy. For some reason, raising an animal can help a child's earlier cognitive development. Pet-owning children also scored higher in several areas of testing.

A dog offers to parents many "teachable moments." These experiences for a child involve emotions, responsibilities, and consequences. When a child follows through with a task, his dog responds.

Most children turn to their pets when they're upset. They're not only a comfort for the child but many dogs sense the change in moods and respond accordingly. ❧

You've Got to Be Kidding!

My dog is usually pleased with what I do, because she is not infected with the concept of what I "should" be doing.

Lonzo Idolswine

Sheffield, my golden retriever, had a cancerous tumor on his thyroid. The blood tests indicated the tumor possibility so I took him to Veterinary Nuclear Imaging Center for a thyroid scintigraphy (thyroid scanning). Sheffield was glad it wasn't a *CAT* scan! The tests confirmed he had cancer so he went in for treatment, which was the injection of radioactive iodine. Sheffield had to stay at the clinic for two weeks in isolation. Other dogs and people had to stay away from him because he was radioactive—he was "hot." After two weeks, I arrived to pick him up. Boy, was he happy to see me.

Before we left, the vet tech gave me some instructions. Sheffield needed to stay away from small children for a week. That sounded all right. He needed to go potty away from other dogs for a couple of weeks. That, too, sounded all right. But the next instruction was a surprise. The tech said, "Now keep in mind it will take a while for all of the radioactivity to dissipate from Sheffield, so you'll need to pick up all of his droppings for the next six weeks and keep them in a container until all the radioactivity is gone."

I looked at him in silence. Finally I said, "You've got to be kidding."

He said, "Nope… you don't want other animals

exposed to it and officials check the garbage dumps with equipment to detect radioactivity and then track down the source." To top it off, he said this with a smile. I looked at Sheffield—he was smiling, too!

"But we're moving 140 miles away in two weeks!"

He replied, "So, take it with you."

"Do you want to come home with me and tell my wife?"

He said (again with a smile), "Not on your life."

We went home and I told Joyce. She stared at

me like I'd lost my mind (again!). Finally, she spoke, "It's not riding with me in the car!"

Well, we took it with us from Long Beach to Bakersfield. I should say the moving van took it. It was a small green Tupperware-type container sealed again and again with duct tape. It looked harmless. I guess it was. But every now and then I thought I saw the truck glowing. It was probably just my imagination. But then again… ❧

By George, He's Got It!

My name is George. You laugh at that? George isn't a name for a dog? Who says? And by the way, what's *your* name? Is that any name for a human? Well, let's not go there. I'm a schnauzer, but not just any schnauzer. I have six American Kennel Club titles, two Obedience Trial Championships, four world records, and four hundred first places in competitions. And if that isn't enough, at the U.S. Police Canine Competition, I'm the only dog in the history of that event to find 47 out of 47 bombs in a week's worth of trials. Yes, I guess I'm proud of these achievements. But I kept thinking there's got to be more to life than this, even a dog's life. And then one day the medical profession came calling. My life changed and so did the lives of several people,

uh, I mean humans, or whatever they call themselves.

It seems a dermatologist was detecting melanomas with his handheld microscope, but wondered if there was a better way to come up with an early detection procedure.

So he came to me. Me! George, the dog! He brought tumor samples and taught me to distinguish the smell of melanoma from benign cancers and normal skin. I learned to nudge the test tubes that held the cancer. And just like the other tasks and competitions that I'd won, *sigh*, I excelled. I got up to a 99 percent accuracy rate for identifying the cancer in the test tubes. Remember the old saying, "Let George do it?" Well, they did.

But then they took me to a medical facility for a big challenge—I had to smell some patients. Humans, yet! I found six melanomas they couldn't detect by their microscopes. Wow! Now I felt fulfilled.

You may wonder how I, George (and most of my canine friends), am able to do this. I'm so glad you asked. They say, "the canine nose knows." It's true. My nose has a few more aroma receptors than yours. You've got, oh between 5 to 15 million. Me? I have about 250 million. So very little slips by me. I can detect certain odors with 10 million times more sensitivity than humans. Isn't that great? Well, I know six people who think so. They're still alive because of my nose. That's something to be thankful for. 🐾

Lonely No More

One of the ways a dog enriches our lives is found in the word *companionship*. It's a togetherness that's constant and not dependent upon the ups and downs of life. Our dog goes where we go, lives where we live, and may even sleep where we sleep.

The word *companion* comes from the Latin *com* meaning "with" and *panis* meaning "bread." This forms *companion* which is literally a meal mate. That's you and your dog sharing life together.

A dog is a constant companion unlike children who grow up, become independent, and move on in life. Your dog will spend his or her entire life with you. And in contrast to your human friends, this companion will have a consistent mood toward you. If you're sick, your dog is there. If you're upset or depressed, it doesn't repel your dog nor do they "catch it" from you. You can hug these companions for hours and they never tire from it.

Dogs also draw others into your life such as human companions. Imagine yourself walking into a room where you don't know a soul. People are involved talking with their friends. Several look your way and a few might say "Hi," but for the most part that's about it. Now walk into that room with your dog and you won't be by yourself for long. Dogs are people magnets.

For example, my wife and I were taking a walk in the mountains where the homes were quite nice. As we walked down one street, we passed by a home having a Christmas boutique (unfortunately!) and Joyce said, "Oh, I want to go in. It will just be a minute." (I knew what that meant!) Fortunately, we had our three-month-old golden retriever with us so that excused me from having to go inside. I sat outside on a stone wall. I couldn't believe several things—the number of women who were coming to this home and the fact that every one made a detour to come over and fuss over Sheffield. When Joyce came out some time later, there was a crowd of ladies around us. I think she knew it wasn't me that attracted all that attention (fortunately).

With a dog you'll end up meeting and talking with more people than you can imagine. What an antidote for loneliness! 🐾

Heaven Only Knows

I love a dog. He does nothing for political reasons.

WILL ROGERS

Dogs don't have souls so far as we know; I therefore have no mandate for saying whether they will or will not go to heaven. But I have to trust God's kindness that there's something I don't know that makes provision for that.

The love dogs give to humans somehow cannot be lost into nothingness. The fact that He created such a beautiful thing as a dog is very obviously part of His pattern and plan for our joy and the joy of humanity.

FATHER JOHN ANDREW

Heart Medicine

Would you believe a doctor writing a prescription for a dog? No, not for the dog to take to a pharmacy to be filled. The prescription the doctor wrote was for a patient stating she needed to acquire a dog for her health. It's really true. A cardiac doctor noticed many of his patients were coming in each week even though they only needed to come in once a month. Many of them just seemed lonely and wanted companionship.

The suggestion was made, "Have you thought of getting a pet?" Most of the time the response was, "My landlord, neighbors, family, spouse, wouldn't permit me to do that."

But when the doctor said, "What if I wrote you a specific prescription?" The response was, "Now, that would probably make all the difference in the world." Many doctors are following this example. These new pet owners are no longer lonely! ❧

Joy in the Moment

Your dog can teach you how to live. Listen to the story of one dog's legacy.

Keesha, a shepherd-malamute mix, was my friend, my confidant, my angel, and ultimately, my teacher. I first began writing about Keesha and her powerful healing lessons while I was recuperating from radiation treatments for aggressive, metastatic neck cancer. Only thirty-seven when I was initially diagnosed with cancer and underwent treatments, it was Keesha's wonderful example of living with an illness that I chose to follow during my year-long course.

When I was in the first stages of cancer, what I valued most were my memories of Keesha's complete and graceful acceptance of every part of her own illness and debilitation. One incident in particular had a profound impact on me, and even more so years later. Several weeks before her death, Keesha had become quite weak from her disease. The long, daily strolls along the marsh near our home became shorter and slower as her cancer spread. In her healthier days, Keesha's greatest joy had been to swim in the deep lagoons filled with cattails and marsh grass. But now, too frail to swim, she looked to the glossy, shallow pools of rain that peppered our streets. At every opportunity, Keesha would plop into a big puddle and splash and bark for as long as I'd let her. The look on her face during those times was the look of a hog in a wallow. On our last excursion together, she was only days away from death, yet she was in bliss.

From a dog splashing in a rain puddle, I learned about choice. Regardless of how much time I had left, I could choose to celebrate whatever possibilities life had to offer me each moment. Or, I could curl up and die. We, the Initiated, can be possessed by a manic sense of urgency and dread unknown to most people. It is a curse and a blessing. The urgency keeps your priorities straight, but it can paralyze momentum and cripple

one's best efforts with fear. The antidote to that fear is to practice joy in the moment.

Joy in life is an option, a choice. It can occur during times of trial as well as sorrow. With a dog, the simple wag of a tail may be the only expression we need to remind ourselves to celebrate as Keesha did. 🐾

Mitzi & Mr. Rogers

I think dogs are the most amazing creatures; they give unconditional love. For me they are the role model for being alive.

GILDA RADNER

In 2003 Mr. Rogers, a favorite of children and parents for decades, passed away. He had a great love for animals. Here is his tribute to a scruffy dog who changed his life as a young kid...

When I was little and didn't have a sister yet, I did have a dog whose name was Mitzi. I got her as a present for taking some terrible-tasting medicine. My parents had promised me a dog if I took the medicine, so I took it without a fuss.

Mitzi was a brown, wire-haired mongrel, and for a long time I think she really was my best friend. In each other's company, we learned about the world. We explored our neighborhood and beyond. I remember feeling a little braver whenever Mitzi was with me. We shared times of particular excitement, joy, and sadness. We both got scared when there was thunder and lightning and often crawled under the bed and quivered together.

When Mitzi died, I was very sad. For a long time afterward I played with a stuffed toy dog pretending it would die and then come back to life, over and over again. Only little by little did I stop playing out that drama.

My friendship with Mitzi was like the friendship that many children have with their pets. My mother and father thought it was "good" for me to have a dog for a companion. Well, it was good for me, but it was only many years after she died that I began to understand how good it was and why. ❧

No Complaining

My dog, Clay, and I are getting old and arthritic. In dog years, Clay's a lot older than me and maybe he's more arthritic, too (at least I can still climb upon the bed without being boosted). My arthritis is the mild kind that moves around from my left hip to my fingers to the heel of my right foot, with just enough pain to make me complain about it. And that's exactly what I was doing—complaining—to a friend of mine recently when she said, "Why can't you be more like your dog?"

I couldn't tell whether she was being serious or sarcastic—or both. "Meaning what?" I asked.

"Well, does Clay complain about *his* arthritis?"

I've been watching Clay lately, and there's something to my friend's comment. On our long walks in the morning, Clay will trot ahead of me, his ears at half-alert, the soles of his paws flicking back like the hooves of a race-horse, his tail swinging pleasurably from side to side, when suddenly, without any warning, those old legs of his will give way and he'll go crashing down into the dirt, a startled look of noncomprehension in his eyes. I'll rush to help him but before I can get there, he'll be up again and back on the trail, his tail swinging pleasurably as though nothing had happened. Not complaining. Not feeling sorry for himself.

Come on, Van, take a tip from your old dog, Clay. Stop complaining, get up, and get on with the joyous business of living! ❧

An Inside Look

Any animal can serve as a teacher; however, our companion animals—the ones who share our daily lives—offer us a lifetime of learning experiences as we watch them grow, thrive, fail, and die.

These animals who share our homes and our work have an uncanny and unparalleled way of seeing through all our false layers, allowing our more genuine selves to emerge. When we are alone with our animal companions, we don't bother with the masks and performances, the armoring and the pretense that we cultivate and display for our loved ones, friends, and enemies. Around our animals, we are our truest selves. When our guard is down, our defenses soften and we can gently open ourselves to receive love, affection, friendship, and insight. ❧

Living by Example

Have you ever thought of your dog as someone who teaches you how to live your life in a better way? Well, it's true. Interestingly enough, your dog is a walking (four-legged) example of how Scripture tells you to live. Many people live their lives dominated by their past. They moan and groan over past mishaps and mistakes allowing them to cloud their present experiences. They seem to forget the apostle Paul's teaching of, "forgetting the past."

We also tend to worry about the future…where we're going, what we're doing and when. In the Bible Jesus said, "Therefore I tell you, do not worry about your life, what you will eat or drink; or about your body, what you will wear. Is not life more important than food, and the body more important than clothes? Look at the birds of the air, they do not sow or reap or store away in barns, and yet your heavenly Father feeds them. Are you not much more valuable than they? Who of you by worrying can add a single hour to his life?"

We end up preoccupied by the past and the future. You wouldn't find a dog being concerned about either one. Their attention is focused on the present, on the delight of the moment. They love where they are at the time. They don't allow the alternatives to distract them from experiencing the here and now. Perhaps we miss the blessings of "now" because of preoccupation with what has been or what could be. You'd never catch a dog doing that. He's too smart for that. ❧

A Breed Apart

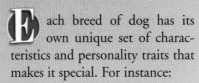

A Pekingese is not a pet dog; he is an undersized lion.

A. A. MILNE

Each breed of dog has its own unique set of characteristics and personality traits that makes it special. For instance:

- An Airedale believes that an object is of no use to anyone unless it provokes a furor.

- Each year, a healthy Jack Russell terrier consumes one and a half times his weight in human patience.

- Bulldogs display that typically English characteristic for which there is no English name.

- All poodles act as if they have won first prize in the lottery of life.

- All spaniels have a way of getting the answer "yes" without ever having posed any clear question.

- The Chihuahua's greatest ambition is to live in a hot country and watch its master throw stones in the sea.

- Golden retrievers are not dogs—they are a form of catharsis.

- The beautiful and elegant Afghan hound knows two things: first, it is not very smart; second, it doesn't matter.

Doggy Dentist

There's a Southern California dentist who owns three little Maltese dogs, but doesn't leave them at home. He takes them to his office. His young clients actually look forward to their visits with him. They have such a good time that the one ingredient kids and adults alike usually take with them to the dentist—fear—is left outside the door. They're not afraid. Why? This dentist allows the children to hold one of his dogs while they sit in his chair and he performs whatever work is needed. Now I could go for that arrangement! 🐾

Lovable Distractions

> *A dog makes the atmosphere safe for emotions, for the expression of the feelings that flow within us. Whatever you're feeling, you can express around your dog. You don't have to censor yourself around your dog as you do around others.*
>
> DR. MARTY BECKER

September 11 changed our lives in so many ways. People came from all over the country to help at Ground Zero. Mike MacIntosh, a pastor and sheriff's chaplain, spent many months assisting those in need at the site. It was exhausting and emotionally draining work. He, too, learned something about life from a dog.

I came across a man and a woman, their two dogs were lying on the ground in front of their bench. Both dogs wore vests. I asked the couple if I could help them in any way. As we talked, I knelt and began patting the dogs and stroking their chins as I would with my two dogs. I was reminded of my dogs and how much they loved to be taken for a run in the park with me. The man explained that they had just flown in from Portland, Oregon, and were looking for a place to serve. "I was born and raised in Portland," I said.

"We have these two compassion dogs and feel we could be of service to someone."

That roused my curiosity, "What's a compassion dog?"

The woman answered, "They're trained to just love people and let people love them. We take them to convalescent and children's hospitals and any place people need comfort and love."

I understood. And the longer I knelt there petting these precious animals, the more I understood. I found my stress evaporating, released by loving these two dogs. Before I said goodbye to them, I actually felt relaxed. I also felt God at work again.

Those two travel-weary dogs taught me a great lesson. When you're worn out there's always enough time to take a break. It is important for us to get back to our old routines. Even if that routine contains a simple walk with your dog. When the rubble is stacked, tangled, and confusing in front of us, the very sight of it can be overwhelming. Staring up at all of that chaos of unfinished business can depress us. We need distractions of love to remind us that things will return to normal at some point in the future. You may discover that ultimately it's those little love-distractions of life that make your life worth living. ❖

Did You Know...

Were you aware that a Newfoundland dog turned the tide of history? Well, it's true. And it's not because of this dog's size, but his instinctual drive to save people and his ability to swim. In 1815, a man was returning to France after being exiled on an island. Impatient and eager to return home, he was pacing the docks waiting for his ship. But it was slippery and he fell into the sea. The Newfoundland was sitting on a boat near the dock and when he saw the incident, he leapt in, grabbed the man by the collar, and took him to shore.

The man's name? Napoleon. If this dog had not responded as he did, the man could have drowned—and the Battle of Waterloo may never have occurred.

Have you ever wondered how seeing-eye dogs got their job? It actually happened by accident. In the early 1900s, a doctor in Germany was walking a blind man through the streets near his hospital when an emergency arose and he had to leave immediately. He left his German shepherd in charge of his blind patient. When he returned, the two of them were still together. He began to wonder about the possibilities and began a training program for dogs as guides for the blind. However, this really wasn't the first occurrence. Archeological evidence suggests a king in Europe used dogs as guides in 100 B.C. There is also a fresco of a dog leading a blind man that was discovered on the wall of a house in Pompeii. It had been buried for centuries by the volcanic eruption in A.D. 79.

Today we have dogs who serve in many service capacities including hearing-guide dogs, therapy dogs, and canine companions for the disabled who can perform 89 different tasks. ❧

How Embarrassing!

They are better than human beings because they know but do not tell.

Emily Dickinson

Would you believe the Cat of the Year honor given by the Westchester Cat Show in New York went to a...dog? In 1998 the award, which is usually given to a cat who displays unusual courage, determination, will to live, or other special quality, was given to Ginny, a schnauzer-Siberian mix. It seems that the canine roams the roads and alleys where she lives looking for stray cats, especially those who are hurt, hungry, or scared. She picks them up and takes them home. It seems her owner finds homes for needy cats. Because of Ginny's efforts, hundreds of cats have been placed, including a deaf cat, a one-eyed cat, and one with no hind feet.

All Ginny asks in return is don't tell her dog buddies about this. It could ruin her reputation as a dog. 🐾

In Loving Memory...

RIVER PINES FLAME OF SHEFFIELD
September 3, 1990 - December 31, 2002

*'Tis sweet to hear
the watch-dog's
honest bark
Bay deep-mouthed
welcome as we
draw near home;
'Tis sweet to know
there is an eye
will mark
Our coming, and
look brighter
when we come.*

LORD BYRON

I went shore fishing the other day and took a friend with me. In fact, I went more for him than for myself. He hadn't been fishing in a while. You see, he's getting old. It's harder to get around and his hearing is going as well. He was quite excited when I told him we were going to the lake. The shore was easier for him than sitting in my old junk boat I keep at the reservoir.

We walked out an old weed-filled road to the dam because bass had been schooling there recently. I was bent on getting out there to fish, but my friend seemed to take his time, noticing the foliage and wildlife around us. I took a cue from him, slowed down, and saw what I'd been missing.

When we got to the dam, we sat down and I began casting out over the sloping bottom. I alternated between a purple worm and a green fleck Yamamoto spider jig. My friend just sat on a towel on the dam content to watch me catch and release a dozen bass and rattle on about nothing significant. I probably repeated stories he'd heard before, but it didn't bother him like it does some people. Now and then he'd get up and come over to take a closer look at a bass I'd caught. Of course, he's seen many fish in his time. He's even had some fish slap him in the head as they were lifted into the boat.

As we walked the half-mile back to the car, I noticed how his pace had slowed. He seemed weary and it was more of an effort to get into the van. I told him to just take a rest while we drove back to my house. We didn't need to talk. I wondered how many more times he'd be able to go fishing with me. I guess we just take it for granted that we'll always be able to go fish. Have you ever wondered about that? Most of us just assume nothing will change. I know that one day he won't be able to go—I don't look forward to that day at all.

He's an excellent sight fisherman. He can spot a bass near the shoreline or next to a rock that I've missed. And he'll stay with that fish until it's caught. What's great about him is the fact he usually gives me the first opportunity to catch it. Once in a great while he gets a bit impatient and goes for it himself. He's also got an uncanny ability to spot crawdads and other critters under the water.

I've learned a lot from him these last few years…I've still got more to learn. My fishing buddy has touched my life in other ways as well.

He came into my life about eight months after my son died. For both my wife and me, he was a source of comfort during our journey through grief. But we weren't the only ones he's helped. A few years later when my mom was spending her last two months in a convalescent home, I'd visit each day and I took my friend with me. He connected so well with the other residents that some of them would sit in the lobby for hours waiting to see him. And when they did, their faces, which most of the time had no expression, would brighten and a rare smile emerged. Several would congregate around him. His gentle touch and silent presence brought delight, comfort, and a bright spot into their day of drab routine. He'd smile at each one and either put his head or a paw in their lap.

Sometimes I'd share stories with them about how my friend would stalk turtles or crawdads in my small backyard pond. One day he was putting his head under the water up to his ears so I put a snorkel on him and took a series of pictures. They laughed when they thought of a 75-pound golden retriever with a snorkel.

A dog for a friend? Oh, yes! Sheffield's more faithful, loyal, patient, and fun-loving than a lot of people I know—as well as never-tiring of fishing with me.

🐎 🐎 🐎 🐎 🐎

Most of the above was written for the conclusion of a book I had coming out in the fall of 2002. I didn't know if my friend would still be with me or not. When it was released, he was. But then his health began to deteriorate. He seemed to rally after his cancer treatment, but after Christmas each day became more difficult for him.

The day started out as any other day. Sheffield raised his head to look around but then slowly lowered it back to the ground. He thumped his tail a couples of times as a greeting, but even that seemed to be too much effort. When he did get up, he just stood there as though he was in a daze. Later that morning, I called him to the front door to see if he wanted to go out and get the paper. He took a few faltering steps and then hesitated as though he didn't know which direction to go. Slowly he moved to the paper, lowered his head, and picked it up. He barely made it to the door before he stopped. It appeared as if he were totally exhausted. Finally, he gave his tail a wag and dropped the paper.

Sheffield had retrieved the paper thousands of times through the years and he always brought it in to me with a sense of

pride. Sometimes when he approached the paper, he would stop and look up and down the street to see who was watching. The only day of the week that he grumped a bit about the task was Sunday. On that day, the *Los Angeles Times* usually weighed more than seven pounds! But he always came through, just like he did this day. Sadly, we both knew it would be the last time.

That evening I sent him out to the yard to relieve himself. When he got outside, he just laid down and rested his head on his paws. He seemed immobile. I walked him to the house where he flopped down on the deck. His breathing was ragged and short. We thought maybe he was going to die right there. But, he rallied and eventually walked to the room where he slept.

The next morning his breathing was worse and he could only walk a few feet. For as long as I can remember, Sheffield would come into my study in the morning and lie on the floor while I had my devotions. This morning I reversed the procedure. I brought my Bible and devotional books into his room, sat on the floor next to him, placed one hand on his back, and then read and prayed. It was both a difficult time, for I knew what was coming, but also a special time.

Joyce and I knew we needed to take him to the vet. We placed Sheffield on a towel and lifted him into the van. When we arrived, two of the vet's assistants brought out a gurney, placed him on it, and took

him in. We waited in one of the rooms and almost immediately the vet came in to tell us he was just about gone. He could prolong his life for a brief time, but we said, "No, it's time."

We had been saying goodbye for several days, but went in for one final farewell. I'm not sure if he was conscious or not. There was a tube down his throat and it was apparent he would be gone within a few minutes. That December 31st was one of the longest days of my life. Just as the memories of a significant person who is gone elicit tears, so do pictures and memories of Sheffield.

We were fortunate to have so many understanding friends. The flowers and cards we received just validated our feelings that Sheffield had touched the lives of more people than we realized.

Sheffield taught us about friendship, faithfulness, loyalty, patience, and love. It was his impact upon our lives that was the inspiration for the book *A Friend Like No Other*. We thank God for Sheffield being a member of our family. We will miss him greatly. ❧

Acknowledgments

"Dog on the Street Interview" is adapted from *Hi. It's Me, Your Dog* by Lisa Mendoza (Clovis, CA: Quill Drive Books, 2000), pp. 88-89.

"Dogged Determination" is adapted from *When Your World Falls Apart* by Mike MacIntosh (Colorado Springs, CO: Cook Communications, 2002), pp. 97-98.

"Sincerely Yours" is adapted from *Dogs Never Lie About* by Jeffrey Moussaieff Masson (New York: Three Rivers Press, 1997), p. 31.

"George the Paperdog" is adapted from *What My Dog Has Taught Me About Life* by Gary Stanley (Tulsa, OK: Honor Books, 1999), pp. 68-70.

"Pet Therapy" is adapted from *Health Benefits of Animals* (Renton, WA: Delta Society, 1995), Vol. 13, No. 3.

"Move It!" is adapted from *The Healing Power of Pets* by Dr. Marty Becker with Danelle Morton (New York: Hyperion, 2002), p. 114.

"If You Want Brighter Children, Get a Dog" is adapted from *The Healing Power of Pets* by Dr. Marty Becker with Danelle Morton (New York: Hyperion, 2002), pp. 27, 29, 33.

"By George, He's Got It!" is adapted from *The Healing Power of Pets* by Dr. Marty Becker with Danelle Morton (New York: Hyperion, 2002), pp. 91-93.

"Lonely No More" is adapted from *Living with Dogs* by Henry and Mary Ellen Korman (Berkeley, CA: Wildcat Canyon Press, 1997), pp. 23-39.

"Heart Medicine" is adapted from *The Healing Power of Pets* by Dr. Marty Becker with Danelle Morton (New York: Hyperion, 2002), pp. 74-75.

"Joy in the Moment" is adapted from *Animals as Teachers and Healers* by Susan Chernak McElroy (New York: Ballantine Books, 1996), pp. 15-16.

"Mitzi & Mr. Rogers" is adapted from *The Dogs of Our Lives* by Louise Goodyear Murray (Secaucus, NJ: Carol Publishing Co., 1995), p. 156.

"No Complaining" is adapted from *Dog Tales: Lessons in Love* by Van Warner (Nashville, TN: Guideposts Dimensions for Living, 1995), pp. 93-94.

"An Inside Look" is adapted from *Animals as Teachers and Healers* by Susan Chernak McElroy (New York: Ballantine Books, 1996), pp. 13-14.

"A Breed Apart" is adapted from *What Do Dogs Know?* by Susan Chernak McElroy, (New York: Free Press, 1997), p. 49.

"Lovable Distractions" is adapted from *When Your World Falls Apart* by Mike MacIntosh (Colorado Springs, CO: Cook Communications, 2002), pp. 96-97.

"Missing Our Dogs," from *The Dogs of Our Lives* by Louise Goodyear Murray (Secaucus, NJ: Carol Publishing Co., 1995), p. 8.

Missing Our Dogs

Old men miss many dogs.
They only live a dozen years, if that.
And by the time you're sixty, there are several.
The names of which evoke remembering smiles.
You see them in your mind, heads cocked and seated.
You see them by your bed, or in the rain.
Or sleeping by the fire by nights
And always dying.

You are young but they are old. They go,
The German shepherd and the poodle,
The basset hound and mutt.
They are remembered like departed children
Though they gave vastly more than they ever took.
And finally you're seeing dogs that look like them.
They pass you in the street but never turn
Although it seems they should, their faces so familiar
Old men miss many dogs.

—STEVE ALLEN